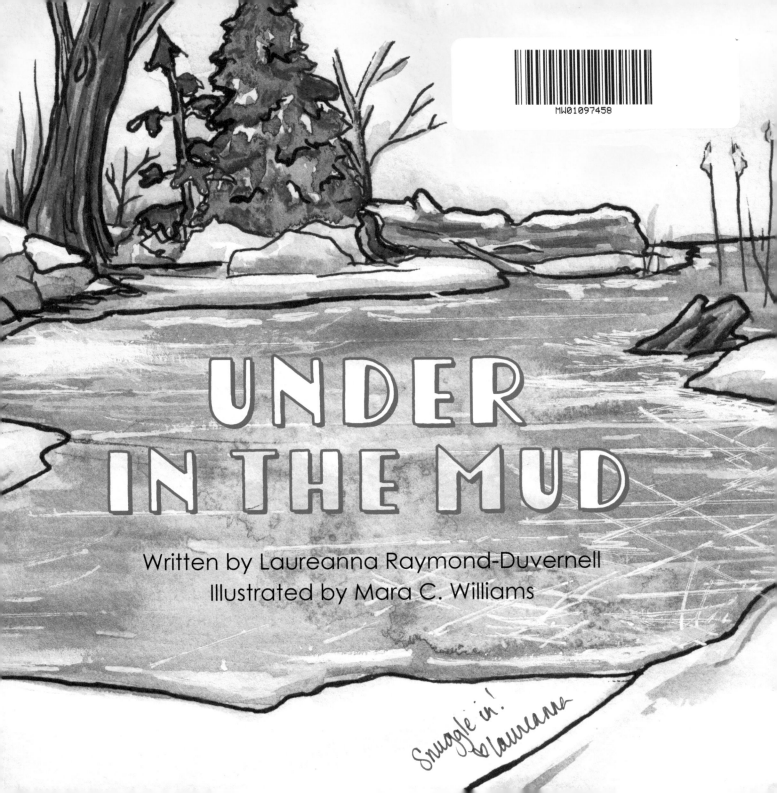

UNDER
IN THE MUD

Written by Laureanna Raymond-Duvernell

Illustrated by Mara C. Williams

Snuggle in!
Laureanne

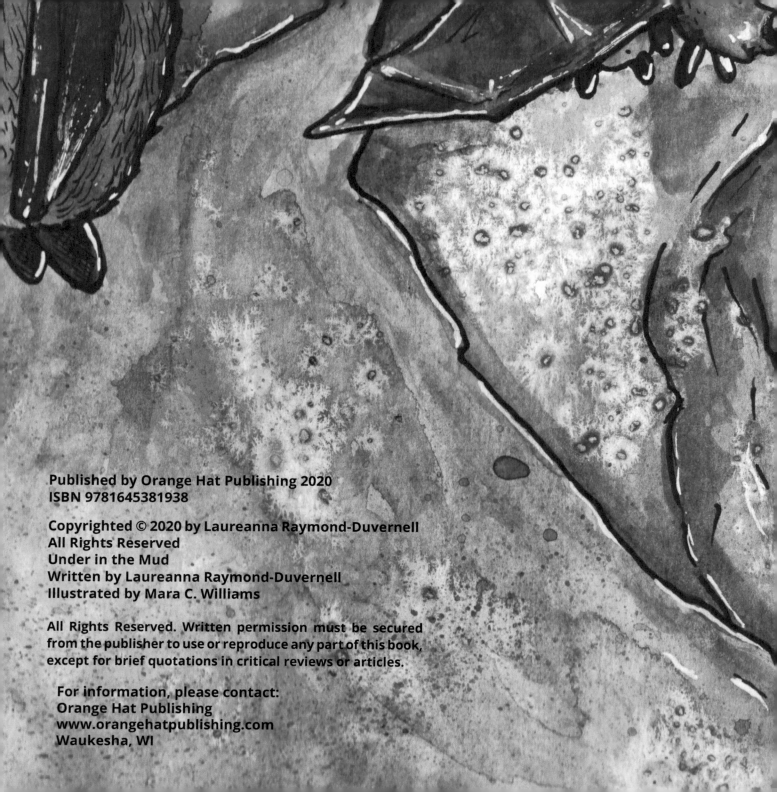

Published by Orange Hat Publishing 2020
ISBN 9781645381938

For information, please contact:
Orange Hat Publishing
www.orangehatpublishing.com
Waukesha, WI

For Sierra and Marina,
my mud monsters
- LRD

For my parents,
Reed and Suzy Williams
- MCW

Under in the mud,
Where the stream used to run,
Sleeps a frozen spring peeper
All alone, just the one.
     "Spring!" dreams the peeper.
     "Ah, spring!" dreams the one.
Frozen in the mud
Where the stream used to run.

In a crack in the rocks,
Small enough to slip through,
Slides a large garter snake
And her snake partners two.
    "Coil!" hisses the snake.
    "We coil!" hiss the two.
So they coil all together
In the rocks they slipped through.

Nestled in leaves,
In a sturdy oak tree,
Sits a fuzzy gray squirrel
And her baby squirrels three.
    "Munch!" chirrs the squirrel.
    "We munch!" chirr the three.
So they munch on acorns
In their nest in the tree.

Deep beneath the ice,
In a pond far from shore,
Floats a silent painted turtle
And his turtle friends four.
        "Breathe..." thinks the turtle.
        "We breathe..." think the four.
So they breathe, still and slow,
In their pond far from shore.

Clustered together,
In a man-made hive,
Hides a large queen bee
And her worker bees five.
"Shiver!" hums the queen.
"We shiver!" hum the five.
So they shiver 'round their queen
In their man-made hive.

Swimming under ice,
To a den made of sticks,
Live a mom and pop beaver
And their beaver kits six.
"Gnaw!" bark the parents.
"We gnaw!" bark the six.

So they gnaw and they nibble
From their den made of sticks.

Up above the clouds,
Where the sun feels like heaven,
Flies a Canada goose
And his goose family seven.
    "Hurry!" honks the goose.
    "We hurry!" honk the seven.
So they hurry to the south
Where the sun feels like heaven.

Over in the woods,
In a nest built too late,
Rests a cold field mouse
And her mouse babies eight.
    "Huddle!" cries the mouse.
    "We huddle!" cry the eight.
So they huddle to stay warm
In their nest built too late.

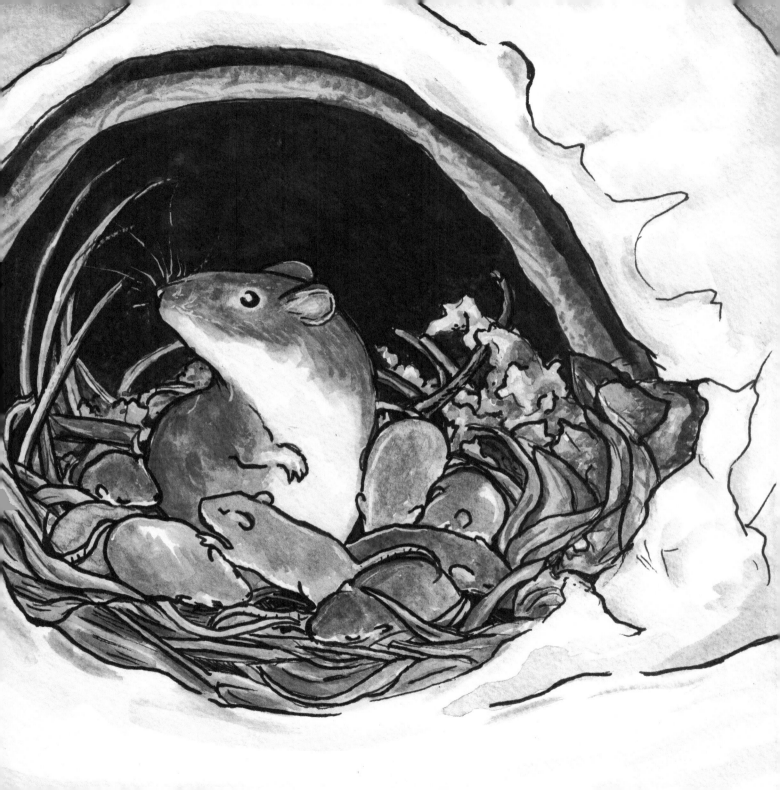

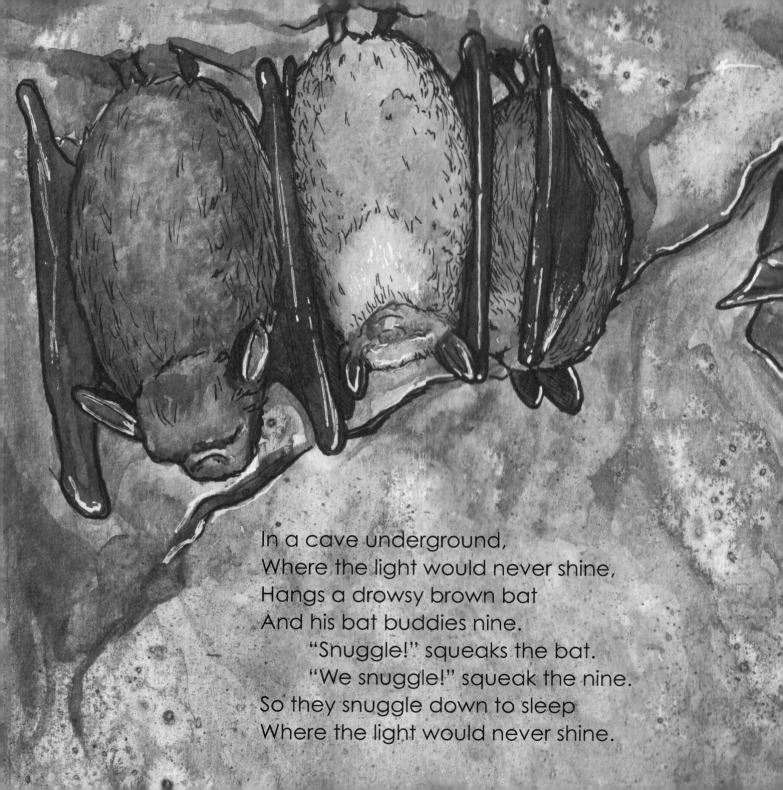

In a cave underground,
Where the light would never shine,
Hangs a drowsy brown bat
And his bat buddies nine.
　　"Snuggle!" squeaks the bat.
　　"We snuggle!" squeak the nine.
So they snuggle down to sleep
Where the light would never shine.

Relaxing by the fire,
In our cozy family den,
Are my family and me
And my best friends ten.
    "Hygge…" I smile.
    "Hygge…" smile the ten.
So we relax in contentment
In our cozy family den.

SPRING PEEPER

When the temperature drops below 32° Fahrenheit, the spring peeper's body produces special sugars that keep the organs inside the frog alive. The frog's cells have less water in them, which means that the animal won't turn into a frogsicle. But spring peepers still need an insulating layer over them (like a blanket), so snow cover, leaves, or mud are good places for them to spend the winter.

GARTER SNAKE

Garter snakes gather with others of their kind during the winter. They will find hibernation dens between rocks, animal burrows, hollow stumps, abandoned buildings—really anywhere that they are protected from the weather. Many garter snakes, sometimes tens or hundreds of them, will coil together to keep warm during the winter.

GRAY SQUIRREL

Gray squirrels stay active during the winter. A pile of leaves wedged in an empty winter tree might be a squirrel drey! There might even be a squirrel living inside. Squirrels rely on the nuts that they have collected and hidden throughout the year to stay alive. Female squirrels can have a litter of babies in the winter, so they need extra food sources to care for their young.

PAINTED TURTLE

Painted turtles are the superstars of the hibernation world. They lay inactive on the bottom of ponds and slow their heart rate to almost completely stopped. Just like the spring peepers, they flood their cells with sugars so that ice can't form in them. And the weirdest part? If they don't have access to oxygen, they can absorb it from the water through their butts. Some people call them "butt breathers"!

HONEYBEE

Honeybees are also active in the winter, but they stay in one spot inside their hive. There can be thousands of bees in one hive! The honeybees gather around the queen and shiver their wings to generate body heat. In the middle of this cluster, it can be as warm as 93° Fahrenheit. The bees eat honey for energy during the winter, and the cluster moves to stay near their honey cells.

NORTH AMERICAN BEAVER

Beavers have a lot of adaptations, or special body features, which help them survive the winter. They have thick fur that they can make waterproof, and their bodies and tails hold extra fat that they can use when they need energy. They work hard on building up their dens with plants and mud to keep them warm during cold months. Beavers also cut extra branches from trees and store them near their dens so that they can eat them all winter long.

CANADA GOOSE

One of the most common sights in fall is the "V" shape of Canada geese flying. Some of these birds fly long distances—from Canada to the southern USA—some migrate only a little bit south, and some don't migrate at all. They fly during the day and night with their families and take turns at the front of the "V" so the leader doesn't get too tired.

FIELD MOUSE

Mice live in burrows, in tree cavities, or in man-made buildings and are active all winter. The females can have four litters of babies in one winter! This means they need to keep eating to be able to stay warm and to feed and protect their young.

Not all animals survive the winter. If they don't have enough food stored up, if their home is not warm enough, or if they have to leave their home because of predators, they may die. These animals become food for other creatures, so even in death, they are helping others to live.

LITTLE BROWN BAT

Little brown bats hibernate in caves or abandoned mines near where they spend most of their lives. Many bats gather together—sometimes thousands in one hibernacula—and huddle to stay warm while they sleep.

HUMAN

Most humans stay active during the winter, but some migrate to warmer areas also. In colder climates, fireplaces are a popular place to relax with friends or family. Hygge (pronounced hoo-gah) is a Danish word that means a feeling of coziness, contentment, and gratitude. Winter is a good time to take pleasure in the simple things that life can offer, especially time spent with those we love.

CPSIA information can be obtained
at www.ICGtesting.com
Printed in the USA
BVHW020049161220
595431BV00002B/22